Careers in Construction

Plumber

Jeri Freedman

Cavendish Square

New York

Published in 2016 by Cavendish Square Publishing, LLC
243 5th Avenue, Suite 136, New York, NY 10016

First Edition

Website: cavendishsq.com

This publication represents the opinions and views of the author based on his or her personal experience, knowledge, and research. The information in this book serves as a general guide only. The author and publisher have used their best efforts in preparing this book and disclaim liability rising directly or indirectly from the use and application of this book.

CPSIA Compliance Information: Batch #CW16CSQ

All websites were available and accurate when this book was sent to press.

Library of Congress Cataloging-in-Publication Data

Freedman, Jeri, author.
Plumber / Jeri Freedman.
pages cm. — (Careers in construction)
Includes bibliographical references and index.
ISBN 978-1-5026-0982-3 (hardcover) ISBN 978-1-5026-0983-0 (ebook)
1. Plumbing—Vocational guidance—Juvenile literature. 2. Plumbers—Juvenile literature.
3. Construction industry—Juvenile literature. I. Title.

TH6130.F74 2016
696.1—dc23

2015032453

Editorial Director: David McNamara
Editors: Andrew Coddington and Kelly Spence
Copy Editor: Rebecca Rohan
Art Director: Jeffrey Talbot
Designer: Alan Sliwinski
Senior Production Manager: Jennifer Ryder-Talbot
Production Editor: Renni Johnson
Photo Research: J8 Media

The photographs in this book are used by permission and through the courtesy of: Ambient Images/UIG/Getty Images, cover; nahariyani/Shutterstock.com, background used throughout; Pojoslaw/iStock/Thinkstockphotos.com; Lisafx/iStockphoto.com, 4, 49; LianeM/Shutterstock. com, 10; Science & Society Picture Library/SSPL/Getty Images, 17; Hellen Sergeyeva/Shutterstock. com, 23; Smit/Shutterstock.com, 28; Image Source/Getty Images, 32; Goodluz/Shutterstock.com, 39; mstay/Getty Images, 43; Francesco Ruggeri/Getty Images, 51; AndreyPopov/Thinkstock.com, 54; Bartco/iStockphoto.com, 58; GregorBister/Getty Images, 60; christian Lagereek/Thinkstock. com, 68; Milos Stojanovic/Getty Images, 70; Gary Friedman/Los Angeles Times via Getty Images, 73; Ambient Images/UIG via Getty Images, 78; AP Photo/Rich Pedroncelli, 80; Comstock/ Getty Images, 82; AP Photo/Wichita Falls Times Record News, Torin Halsey, 96; Lisa F. Young/ Shutterstock.com, 98; Wipeout 997/File:Greywater Recycling Heat Recovery System 1.jpg/ Wikimedia Commons, 100.

Printed in the United States of America

Table of Contents

Plumbers play a major role in the construction of new buildings by ensuring the proper flow of water through pipes and fixtures.

Introduction

Houses, hospitals, factories, office buildings, and every other building people visit every day were built by hardworking members of the construction industry. Any and all of these buildings include features installed by plumbers. Sinks, toilets, showers, sprinklers, water distribution and waste treatment systems, and pipelines that carry fuel all function because of plumbers. The plumbing trade has been critical to the construction of buildings since ancient times. Today, plumbers play a bigger role than ever before, providing systems to housing and office developments and processing plants that rely on the flow of liquids and gases.

The primary role of a plumber is to install the necessary pipes, valves, and fixtures to keep water flowing in a safe and reliable manner from water supply lines to sinks, faucets, showers, sprinkler systems, and industrial production lines, and back to sewer systems and waste treatment plants. A plumber may perform other specialized tasks, depending on the field of construction he or she works in, and his or her level of experience. A plumber may be hired by a **general contractor** to work as a **subcontractor** on new construction projects, or hired directly by an individual to work on their home or business.

Learning a trade such as plumbing is a way to make a good living if you choose not to attend college. It offers more opportunity for non-college-bound students than merely accepting a job that requires fewer skills. In addition to good pay, the plumbing field provides a career path with a salary that increases as you gain experience and develop more advanced skills. Becoming a plumber can also provide the flexibility to choose the projects you want to work on and the environment in which you work.

The economy has gone through many ups and downs over the years. A young person starting out today is likely to encounter times when there is a downturn in the economy. However, plumbers are always in demand, because even when there are not a lot of new construction projects, existing pipes and fixtures always need to be maintained and repaired. Becoming a plumber can offer job protection and stability in times when the economy is poor.

Those who choose to learn specialized plumbing applications can earn even more than general plumbers. Pipefitters, who specialize in installing gas, oil, or high-pressure steam pipes, work in applications such as energy, chemicals, and industrial processing. As the economy improves and the construction of new homes and businesses increases, the demand for plumbers is likely to increase as well. Although the amount of construction work varies depending on the time of year, plumbers are still needed year-round to repair plumbing systems.

Being a plumber gives you control over your career. You have the option of working on different types of construction. There is a demand for plumbers in residential, commercial, and industrial projects. Plumbers also have a choice of companies to work for. They can choose to work for a small or large plumbing contractor or plumbing services company or even for themselves. The size of the projects on which they work can vary from large housing developments and apartment buildings to factories, schools, and shopping malls. Some specialize in steam or gas pipefitting, and others work as pipefitters on large pipelines carrying natural gas, crude oil, or fuel. If they choose, plumbers can also work on industrial projects overseas.

Working as a plumber requires you to work independently, solve problems, and pay attention to detail to protect yourself and others from accidents and injuries. On one hand, plumbers have to be prepared for hard and sometimes messy work. On the other, because of the skill required and the constant demand, master plumbers can make significant incomes. Many plumbers start out working for a company, but eventually they strike out and start their own businesses.

Although you do not have to go to college to become a plumber, you still need to commit to learning the skills of the profession. Most plumbers start out as apprentices. They are taught the trade by the experienced plumber they work under. This type of learning is suitable for those who prefer a practical education, focused on skills that can be applied directly to earning a living. However, some course-based learning is still required. In order to qualify for a plumber's license, plumbers must complete a number of hours of coursework, which can be taken in a classroom or online. This coursework focuses specifically on technical information used in the trade. Because this study takes place on your own time, you must be able to apply yourself and stay disciplined without supervision.

This book covers the various aspects of plumbing work and what is required to become a plumber. Chapter 1 covers the history of the plumbing industry, explains what plumbing consists of and how it works, and provides an overview of the various types of plumbing construction. Chapter 2 explains what you need to do to become a plumber, including the education and training you require. It also explains the licensing requirements. Chapter 3 describes what life on the job is like for plumbers with different levels of experience. It provides insight into the range of jobs available for plumbers and the activities performed in each specialty field. Chapter 4 offers information on job prospects for the plumbing industry and explains how to go about securing a job in the field. Finally, it takes a look into the future of the plumbing industry and the role likely to be played by the plumber in the years to come.

The Aqueduct of Pegões near Tomar, Portugal, was built during the late sixteenth and early seventeenth centuries. It carried water over 3.5 miles (6 kilometers).

CHAPTER 1

The Plumbing Industry

Plumbing is the system of pipes, fixtures, valves, fittings, and other components used to transport and supply water. Plumbing brings **potable** water for drinking and washing into buildings. It removes water that is dirty or contains waste, and supplies water for steam-based heating systems.

The History of Plumbing

Plumbing dates back thousands of years. Archaeologists have uncovered the remains of plumbing systems in many ancient civilizations, including Greece, Persia, India, and China. These systems were used to bring water into public baths and fountains that provided drinking water, and to remove wastewater. The Minoan-built palace of Knossos on the island of Crete contained terracotta pipes beneath the floor, which carried hot and cold water to faucets and fountains. The city had sewer systems of baked clay that drained off wastewater and rainwater. The first flush toilet was also found in the remains of the palace of Knossos. It consisted of a latrine with a wooden seat and a small reservoir of water that emptied into it. In ancient Mesopotamia (modern-day Iraq) and Egypt, pipes of baked clay were also used to transport water.

The Greeks developed plumbing systems that produced both hot and cold water. The Greek inventor Heron pioneered a pressurized system of pipes to provide water to the city of Alexandria. There is evidence that plumbing was used in ancient China to supply water to public bathhouses. In a Han Dynasty (206 BCE to 24 CE) tomb, a two-thousand-year-old toilet was found. It had a flushing mechanism reliant on running water and a stone seat.

The Romans were the masters of plumbing in the ancient world. They built their first sewers between 800 BCE and 735 BCE. The word "plumbing" comes from the Latin word *plumbum*, which means "lead," because the first pipes used by Romans were made of lead. The Romans were excellent engineers. They created a system of roads that ultimately crossed the known world. They also constructed a series of aqueducts that brought water to Rome from sources located up to 10 miles (16 km) away from the city.

Since Roman pipes were made of lead, which was much more durable than the wood or clay conduits used by many early civilizations, the plumber was a lead worker. Roman plumbers did much the same work that modern plumbers do. They fit and installed pipe, connecting to sewers when necessary to remove waste, and to exterior conduits to bring in drinking water. The ancient Romans built hot-water and steam-producing systems for use in their public bathhouses. In the bathhouse, patrons had a choice of many rooms with different types of baths, from cold to warm to hot, as well as a steambath. Furnaces were built beneath the floors to heat water stored in tanks.

The aqueducts built by the Romans covered 220 miles (354 km). Of that, 190 miles (306 km) of pipe ran underground. The remaining piping was raised overhead. The aqueducts relied on gravity to carry the water from its source into the city. The Roman aqueducts transported about 300 gallons (1,136 liters) per capita of water into the capital.

The Romans set out to conquer the known world. They succeeded in taking control of much of Europe, including France and England. As they traveled across the continent, they brought their technology with them, including plumbing. They established Roman baths at Aquae Sulis, the site of the modern city of Bath in England. With the fall of Rome in the fifth century CE, the Romans withdrew from England. The former Roman provinces in Europe, including England, were overrun by barbarians, and the knowledge of Roman technology was lost.

The rise of Christianity caused a further setback to the development of plumbing technology. The early Christians believed it was a sin to pay attention to the body, instead of focusing on the soul. Therefore, bathing was seen as vain and sinful. The Catholic Church dominated Europe until the Renaissance. During the Renaissance, an interest in plumbing was revived. In the fifteenth century, German ironworkers discovered a way to heat iron to a temperature hot enough to melt it. They could then pour it into castings, or molds, which made it possible to fashion cast-iron objects, including hollow pipes. The first cast-iron plumbing pipes were installed in Siegerland, Germany, in 1455. In the seventeenth century, King Louis XIV of France had a cast-iron plumbing system installed at the palace at Versailles in order to bring water to the palace's fountains from a pumping station 15 miles (24 km) away.

Contrary to popular belief, the toilet was not invented by Thomas Crapper. The first flush toilet was actually invented by Sir John Harrington, Queen Elizabeth I's godson, in 1596. However, the cistern that refilled the toilet required a large amount of water. At that time, people got their water from town pumps and carried it to their houses. Obtaining water to refill the cistern on Harrington's toilet, called a "jakes," was too difficult at a time when there were no pipes bringing water into homes. The toilet failed to catch on.

It was not until the Enlightenment in the seventeenth century that an interest in science and engineering led to a new interest in plumbing technology. The rapid growth of cities in the seventeenth and eighteenth centuries also led to an increased interest in improving water supply and sanitation.

These needs fueled the development of water companies, which competed to bring water to the populace for profit. Between 1609 and 1613, Hugh Myddleton (1560–1631) engineered a series of aqueducts to bring water from Hertfordshire to London. In the process, he founded the New River Company, one of the largest water companies of the time. The Chelsea Waterworks Company was founded in 1723 and brought water from the Thames to parts of London and the surrounding area. Other waterworks companies followed in rapid succession.

In the eighteenth century, the Roman baths in Bath were revived. Richard "Beau" Nash (1674–1761) was a nobleman and gambler. Much like the celebrities of today, he set the standard for what was fashionable. He took up residence in the town of Bath, making it a popular destination. As a result, the Roman baths were resurrected and enhanced. Bath promoted the waters of its spa as having healing powers, and the town flourished.

Prior to the eighteenth century, sewers were open conduits in the street that carried waste to bodies of water. This created a foul stench and contributed to the spread of diseases, such as cholera and typhus, when the local water supply became contaminated. The first underground sewer was constructed in New York City in 1728.

In 1775, Alexander Cumming (circa 1731–1814), a Scottish watchmaker, obtained a patent on the first commercial flush toilet. Cumming's innovative invention of the S-pipe, used below the bowl, kept sewer gas from coming back into the toilet, and made it possible to use a toilet with a sewer system. It was not until the late nineteenth century, however, that the toilet became a commercial success. Thomas Crapper (ca. 1836–1910)

Pedestal Wash=down Closets.
"The Cedric."

No. 178		Section.

No. 178.	"Cedric" W.C., with S. or P. Trap,	Cane and White	...	...	£0 19 6
Do.	do.	Cane and Printed	...	...	1 2 6
Do.	do.	White or Ivory	...	...	1 2 6
Do.	do.	White and Printed	...	...	1 7 6
Do.	do.	White and Decorated	...	...	1 13 0

"The Deluge."

No. 169	No. 170

No. 169.	"Deluge" W.C., with Slop Top.			No. 170.	"Deluge" Closet.		
	Plain Surface ...	...£3	4 6		Plain Surface ...	...£2	2 0
	Raised Ornamentation	3	9 0		Raised Ornamentation	2	6 6

Can be supplied with C.C. Outlets either P or S at same prices.

Paper Boxes, Plain Surface, 7/- ; Raised Ornamentation, 7/9.

This page from the Thomas Crapper and Company catalog shows some of the toilets offered by the company in 1902. "The Cedric" uses the S-pipe design.

did not invent the toilet. However, he owned a company that made plumbing parts, including fittings. He contributed a number of improvements to the toilet, including the floating ballcock, which is the mechanism inside a toilet's tank that allows it to refill automatically after emptying. The combination of direct pipe connections from houses to the sewer system and an easy-to-use tank refilling mechanism finally made toilets viable for common use by the turn of the last century.

It was actually soldiers returning from World War I who are credited with popularizing the term "crapper." Toilets were still relatively new at the time, with outhouses still in common use. Soldiers encountered the Crapper brand name on most of the commodes they encountered overseas in England.

In the 1870s, the first boiler-based indoor heating systems were developed. Pressurized hot water was moved between a boiler and a storage pipe, circulating through a series of pipes. This is the basis of the radiator, or "forced hot water," system of heating.

The first plumbing code in the United States was published in 1928 at the order of Herbert Hoover, when he was secretary of commerce. One of the new technologies to come out of World War II was plastics, artificial materials developed in response to the shortage of metal caused as it was appropriated for military purposes. After the war, plastics continued to find new applications. In 1966, plastic pipe, called PVC (short for polyvinylchloride), began to be used in place of copper pipes for plumbing.

Recent advances in plumbing include the mandating of low-flow plumbing fixtures, such as toilets and faucets, to conserve energy; fiber-optic cameras that allow the internal inspection of installed pipes; **hydrojetting** equipment for drain cleaning; and electronic transmitting units for tracing pipes.

The Principles of Plumbing

Plumbers have a number of different responsibilities. Among these are:

- Providing and maintaining a supply of safe drinking water
- Ensuring safe food storage
- Installing plumbing fixtures, such as toilets and sinks
- Connecting water lines to sewer pipes
- Ensuring the correct airflow in pipes and venting
- Making sure that water flows in and out at the proper speed and doesn't back up
- Testing and inspecting pipes
- Unclogging pipes and cleanouts
- Replacing worn or damaged pipes
- Installing devices for the efficient use of water
- Installing and maintaining hot-water heaters and water-based heating systems

All premises in which people live or work need a supply of potable water. A plumber must make sure that water lines to faucets are hooked up to a safe source of drinking water and that there is no backflow into the line or cross-contamination from other lines in the system. State health departments and the Environmental Protection Agency issue regulations regarding potable water. Ensuring safe food storage means installing proper drains in walk-in refrigerators, freezers, and coolers. These drains need to allow run-off from water that accumulates, to carry water away from food.

Plumbers must know what fixtures are required for a job and how to install them correctly. In residential construction, every house must have at least one toilet, lavatory (bathroom) sink, kitchen sink, and bathtub or shower. Office buildings, schools, factories, and other structures are also required by law to have sufficient sanitary facilities. Plumbers may also install optional fixtures, such as in-sink garbage disposals or whirlpool tubs. All fixtures must be installed with proper **traps**, and in areas with suitable lighting and ventilation. Water heaters must be installed with proper pressure relief valves and drainage tubes to ensure they are safe and won't explode. Gas water heaters must be tested to make sure there are no gas leaks.

All buildings need a drainage system to get rid of used water and waste. Fixtures have to be connected to the public sewer system, in areas that have them. Otherwise, they have to be connected to alternative sewage treatment sources, such as septic tanks. Drainage systems must incorporate a means to circulate air through the pipes, to prevent waste from being sucked back into the lines. To accomplish this, plumbers install vent pipes. These pipes extend through the roof of the building and connect to the plumbing lines, to bring air into the system. Plumbers must make sure that pipes have the proper slope (angle), connections, and supports. Many residential pipes today are made of PVC, which is a lightweight material. However, copper pipes are used in many applications, and older buildings might have lead or even cast-iron pipes. Heavy metal pipes require more support than pipes made of lighter materials.

Plumbers must have extensive knowledge of which materials are safe to use with a given type of pipe. For example, a lye-based drain cleaner should not be used on lead pipes because it reacts with them and produces material that builds up inside pipes and clogs them. When doing renovation work, plumbers must make sure the existing pipes are sound. Some materials, such as iron and **galvanized** steel, used in old pipes can deteriorate.

In addition, some old construction includes lead drains, which can leach lead into the water system. Old pipes often must be replaced with new pipes, which might be made of copper or PVC. Often when old piping is replaced, all the piping is updated. New copper piping can be connected to old galvanized steel piping, but only if special dielectric connections are used.

When piping is installed or repaired, the plumber must perform tests to make sure that he or she identifies any leaks or defects that need to be corrected. When repairing or installing plumbing pipes and fixtures, plumbers must be careful to work in a way that doesn't damage walls, floors, ceilings, or other parts of a building. This doesn't just mean taking care when working with tools and installing pipes, vents, drains, and supports; it also means making sure to avoid water damage from leaking pipes.

As the population of the world has grown, providing enough water for everyone has become a significant concern. Therefore, regulations have been issued at the state and federal level that mandate the use of low-water toilets, faucets, and showerheads, in order to conserve water. Plumbers must use fixtures that comply with these regulations.

Tools of the Trade

Plumbers use hand, power, and electronic tools in their work. They use adjustable pipe wrenches to tighten and loosen the fittings that connect pipes. A less familiar type of wrench is the faucet valve seat wrench. There is a valve in faucets that controls the amount of water that comes out when the handle is turned. When this valve becomes worn, the faucet can leak. The faucet valve seat wrench is used to remove the faulty valve from the faucet, and a faucet valve reseating tool is used to replace it.

These are examples of various pipe fittings used to connect pipes, and components that attach to pipes, such as a showerhead.

Plumbers remove material from clogged toilets by using plungers to create suction. When a plunger is not sufficient to clear a blocked pipe, they use a toilet auger, more commonly referred to as a "snake." This is a device that consists of a cable with an auger bit on one end and a hand crank on the other. The bit end is inserted into a clogged pipe, and the crank is extended. The bit is used to break through the clog or, in some cases, to retrieve an object such as a rag that is clogging the pipe. A related device is the sink auger, which is used to clear clogs in sink pipes. For larger jobs, plumbers use power drain cleaners, which are run by a motor.

Plumbers cut a lot of pipe. To do this, they use a pipe cutter. The plumber clamps the pipe cutter onto a piece of pipe and then spins it around, gradually tightening it, by means of a knob or ratchet, until the cutting blade cuts completely through the pipe. PVC pipe is glued together, but pieces of metal plumbing pipes are **welded** together. Plumbers use a variety of welding torches to accomplish this.

Plumbers also use special materials, such as Teflon tape. This tape is wrapped around the end of one piece of pipe before it is connected to another pipe. It helps the pipes fit together to minimize leaks. Plumbers use a variety of rubber and nylon washers to keep valves in faucets from leaking.

Today's plumbers also use electronic tools to inspect the state of existing pipes and plumbing systems. The pipe inspection camera is a small video camera attached to the end of a cable that is inserted into a pipe. The cable is extended through the pipe, much like a snake-style pipe cleaner, and the camera sends images of the interior of the pipe to a computer monitor. The video inspection system allows plumbers to get a firsthand look at the condition of pipes to locate any problems such as leaks or breaks. Video inspection is used both to evaluate the state of plumbing in buildings and to find leaks or breaks in sewer pipes. The video can be saved on the computer for future reference during the repair phase.

Working as a Plumber

There are different types of plumbers. Residential plumbers work on houses, apartments, and condominiums both while they are being built and after they are finished. When they do construction work, they have to do their work in two phases. They install the pipes that will carry water and waste during the rough-in phase, before the walls are in place. They may also have to do underground and exterior work, laying and connecting pipes to the sewer system and city water supply.

After the walls are in place, they return and install the plumbing fixtures, such as toilets, hot-water heaters, and sinks. Working during the rough stage of construction and during outside jobs, the plumber may have to work in hot, cold, or rainy weather. Plumbers working on new construction must work in areas that are full of construction materials, tools, and equipment. Some of the construction debris can be sharp or hazardous.

Plumbers frequently work in finished residences. They need to fix leaks, replace broken pipes, and clear blockages. After storms, pipes may be damaged or clogged, either in the home or between the house and the sewer or city water lines. Plumbers may also be called to install new or additional fixtures. Frequently, bathrooms need to be renovated, requiring new tubs or showers, toilets, and sinks. Often old plumbing needs to be updated as well. When working on finished residences, plumbers may need to work in crowded cellars or access pipes that run through walls or the ceilings between floors.

Shopping malls, office buildings, restaurants, and shops are examples of commercial establishments. These types of structures often have air, oil, gas, and steam lines in addition to water lines. Unlike a house, which usually has only one boiler, hot-water heater, and the like, commercial facilities often have multiple boilers and other equipment. They also may have special water-filtration systems. All these types of pipe systems are the realm of the plumber. However, if any of these types of lines are under high pressure, such as steam lines, then a type of plumber with specialized training, called a steamfitter, is required.

Industrial plumbers work on plants that process water or chemicals. They also install piping systems in factories that use chemicals or other liquids in their processing. Sometimes they work on sewer, water-processing, or waste treatment plants that service a town or city. These types of projects often require very large and complicated piping systems, and work on them may continue for months or even years. Contracts for these types of projects are often awarded by the government, although sometimes they are completed for privately run for-profit utility companies. Large chemical-processing and oil-refining companies build facilities that incorporate massive piping systems. Industrial plumbing work includes installing piping systems for factories. The type of plumbing systems required by a manufacturing plant depend on the product being manufactured. Factories may need lines that carry air, oil, gases, chemicals, steam, and various types of waste. The plumber may need to install large drains and

SPECIAL TYPES OF PLUMBERS

Within the plumbing industry, there are various specialty plumbers. Among these are:

Pipefitters: Pipefitters install all types of pipe, for both low-pressure and high-pressure applications. They work on construction projects requiring a large amount of piping. Therefore, they do mostly commercial and industrial work.

A pipefitter installs pipes for a heating system. Pipefitters work on pipes of many different sizes and materials.

They also work on heating and air-conditioning systems. In addition to installing pipes, they work with industrial control systems that use computerized-control plumbing systems in industrial and power plant facilities.

Gasfitters: Gasfitters install and repair the lines that carry natural gas to facilities. Natural gas is used in heating systems, but it is also used in industrial applications. This can be a dangerous profession, as natural gas is flammable and explosive.

Steamfitters: Steamfitters are specially trained to install steam pipes. Steam is transmitted through pipes under high pressure. High-pressure pipe systems are used in industrial and commercial facilities to carry oil or gas. In large complexes, high pressure is also used to carry hot water for heating from boilers to points throughout the facility. Working with high-pressure pipe systems is dangerous and requires special training.

Sprinkler Fitters: Sprinkler fitters install facility-wide automatic sprinkler systems. Such systems may contain water, but they may also use other materials, such as gases, designed to deprive fires of oxygen.

pipes, and tanks to dispose of industrial waste. He or she may also need to install special sprinkler and fire hose supply systems.

Working on the construction of a large facility means that plumbers will be working in areas where large construction vehicles and equipment are being operated. Cranes may be moving heavy beams and other material, with large generators producing power for tools and equipment. For their safety, plumbers need to pay attention to where equipment is and what it is doing. In multistory buildings, plumbers may have to work on the upper stories during the rough-in stage of construction. Large construction projects use massive amounts of material. Some of this material, such as insulation, may be dangerous. If a plumber is working in a factory, there may be hazardous chemicals on-site that are used in the production process. Plumbers must understand what material will be in the area where they are working, and take appropriate safety precautions if needed.

Some construction projects—for example, office buildings, apartment complexes, and commercial facilities such as airports, schools, and hospitals— may have to be completed by a certain deadline. If a project is not completed on schedule, the project's general contractor may have to pay a stiff penalty fine.

Therefore, plumbers on those jobs may have to work beyond the normal 8 a.m. to 5 or 6 p.m. workday to complete the required work on schedule.

Many plumbers make a living as **independent contractors,** working for themselves. Others work for a plumbing contractor who runs a small business and employs a number of other plumbers. Plumbers working independently or in plumbing businesses may be hired as subcontractors by general contractors constructing residential or commercial buildings. Many plumbers choose to join the plumbing union. This can give them access to many municipal and larger commercial and industrial jobs.

A master plumber instructs a plumbing apprentice on how to cut and connect pipes.

CHAPTER 2

Becoming a Plumber

Plumbers need to know various types of mathematics. They have to be able to measure both quantities and lengths of pipe, figure out how the pipes will be joined together, and calculate the angles at which the pipes must be placed. They also have to be able to calculate pressures and flow rates to ensure that water flows properly and doesn't backflow. Therefore, geometry and algebra are a necessity. Plumbers must have a thorough knowledge of the National Plumbing Code. This is a series of rules and regulations governing all aspects of plumbing work. A contractor must ensure that any plumbing he or she works on is "up to code." This means that it meets at least the minimum requirements of the National Plumbing Code and conforms to any state and local codes. Learning about the code is included in all training programs for plumbers. The code is updated periodically, so even licensed plumbers need to make sure they stay up to date on changes in the regulations.

Plumbers must have both strength and manual dexterity. They must be able to carry heavy pipes and move appliances during the plumbing process. However, they must also be able to manipulate small connections and components inside devices such as faucets. They must be able to install devices in small spaces and may have to climb to reach overhead pipes when necessary. Industrial plumbers may have to install very large air-conditioning and ventilation units on the roofs of buildings.

Plumbers often choose between different ways to solve a problem. They have to figure out which materials would be most appropriate for a particular job. Therefore, plumbers need to analyze problems in a systematic and logical way. They must be able to focus on the problem and have patience and persistence to work at it until they find the solution. They must also be able to work independently. To make sure that students develop these skills, training programs require them to complete hands-on projects. Doing these projects helps students to apply and practice the skills they will use on the job.

However, you can develop many of these skills while you are still in high school. For example, the papers you write for courses such as English and history require you to organize your thoughts and create logical arguments to support your ideas. Science courses also require you to figure out why things act the way they do. Take advantage of these opportunities to hone your logic and problem-solving skills.

Preparing in High School

If you are interested in becoming a plumber, you might choose to get an entry-level job or enter an apprenticeship program in the plumbing field directly out of high school. In order to succeed in your work and training, you will need math and English skills. Therefore, you will want to make sure you prepare adequately through the classes you take in high school.

General Courses

To repair, install, and modify plumbing components, you will need to do mathematical calculations. Therefore, you need to take math courses in high school, including algebra and geometry. In addition, you should take physics and chemistry courses. Physics will teach you the basic principles that govern the behavior of liquids and gases. Chemistry will allow you to learn how chemicals and materials interact with each other. Today, every field, including the plumbing industry, requires a knowledge of computers. So, if your school offers classes in computing, it is beneficial to take them. In your professional work, you will need to record information on a computer and write reports and bids for jobs, so a class in keyboarding or typing will come in handy.

As a plumber you will have to communicate with customers and other contractors. Therefore, you need to be able to express your ideas clearly and effectively to avoid misunderstandings. Studying English composition and grammar will help you develop good communication skills. Since it is likely that you will be working with people of different ethnic backgrounds on construction projects, knowing a second language can help you on the job and also make you a more attractive job candidate down the road.

Plumbers have to carry heavy pipes and fixtures. As a plumber, you will spend a great deal of time on your feet, and have to climb and work in cramped spaces. Because of the manual nature of plumbing, it is important to be in good physical condition. You should prepare before you become an apprentice to better meet the strenuous demands of the job. Aside from school-based coursework, you might want to take a first aid/cardiopulmonary resuscitation (CPR) course, which is offered by organizations such as the Red Cross and the American

Heart Association. Construction work is dangerous, and this type of course teaches you what to do if someone is injured on the job.

All plumbers begin by learning the basic skills required to be a plumber. They can get this training either on the job or in academic courses. However, those interested in pursuing a particular type of plumbing work often go on to programs offered by schools or professional associations that teach the specific skills required by that area of work.

Vocational and Technical Programs

In some school systems, vocational programs are available at the high school level. Some cities even have dedicated vocational high schools. Enrolling in this type of program prepares students to start working as soon as they graduate. After graduating, students with vocational training can apply for an apprentice program or take a position as a junior-level plumber with a plumbing contractor, who can provide more advanced on-the-job training. The curriculum of a typical vocational program in this area covers all the major areas in plumbing over four years. It covers concepts, but also includes hands-on projects, where students learn practical plumbing techniques. Students study math used by plumbers and learn how to read and draw plumbing diagrams, the rules of the National Plumbing Code, and their state's plumbing code. They learn how to assemble various types of pipe, such as copper, cast-iron, and PVC plastic pipe. They are taught the ways to support pipe, and practice drilling, notching, cutting, and welding. Since installing appliances is a significant part of a plumber's job, students learn to install and repair hot-water heaters, boilers, and tanks. How to install natural gas lines and vent gas chimneys is taught, as well as how to install and repair various types of heating systems. The installation of water pumps, water distribution systems, and waste treatment systems are covered, as well as how to clear blockages. The use of test equipment is also covered. Students are taught safety procedures, including the proper use of both hand and power tools. They will most likely have to complete a series of projects demonstrating their knowledge of different types of plumbing components. Students will also have to complete reading, writing, and math assignments. These are designed to be relevant to the plumbing field. As with any other high school program, students will have to pass quizzes and tests. They may also have to write papers on plumbing topics and/or successfully complete an independent project—usually in their senior year.

Some schools offer vocational programs that include a practical component in which junior and senior students

A student in a vocational program learns how to safely and properly operate equipment.

have the opportunity to work at local businesses as part of their training. This gives them the chance to experience what it is like to work in the field.

Many vocational schools offer business programs as well as training in the trades. If your school has a business program, you should check to see if it is possible to take an accounting class. Although plumbers start out as apprentices and journeymen working for someone else, many plumbers eventually start their own businesses. Having sound business skills, especially in accounting, is important to run a successful company.

Further Education

There are several different ways you can train to become a plumber. You can get a job directly out of high school or go on to get additional vocational education. The approach that is right for you will be affected by which schools in your area offer training programs. The opportunities for training will also vary with the number of plumbers in the area and the amount of construction work. The larger the pool of plumbers and the greater the number of construction projects, the more openings there will be for apprentices.

One option for training to be a plumber is to land a job with a plumbing contractor and train in the field in the practical aspects of plumbing work. Larger plumbing companies may also cover the cost of courses required for licensing as a plumber. However, some plumbing contractors hire only applicants who already have some education from traditional or online vocational training programs. If you study plumbing in vocational school, you can also get a job at a water supply utility or waste treatment facility.

Certificate and Degree Programs

College-level certificate and two-year associate's degree plumbing programs are available from community colleges, standard colleges, and technical institutes. Certificates of training for plumbers provide students with the basic knowledge they need for an apprenticeship. Associate's degree programs provide more in-depth training and cover more advanced types of plumbing systems. This type of knowledge can be useful for students who wish to work in areas such as public works and hydraulic systems. Having a degree can be helpful if you want to eventually work in a supervisory or design position. However, it is always possible to study for an associate's degree part-time or online while working if you reach a point in your career where you feel you need a higher level of education.

Students in plumbing programs learn how to install, maintain, and repair residential, commercial, and industrial plumbing systems. They study how to safely operate hand and power tools, interpret readings from plumbing test instruments, solve mathematical problems related to plumbing, and locate and interpret sections of the National Plumbing Code regulations as they apply to specific jobs. They perform calculations related to specific plumbing installations and are taught to read plumbing diagrams. They learn about water and waste systems, plumbing pipes, and fixtures. Students also study how to plumb appliances and install heating and cooling systems, as well as special equipment. Information on the installation and repair of steam, hot water, and natural gas heating systems is also covered. Students learn to implement the procedures of the OSHA (Occupational Safety and Health Administration) Act, which protect employees in the workplace.

Examples of courses taken by plumbing students include:

- Blueprint Reading and Plumbing Drawings
- First Aid and Safety
- Fixtures, Faucets, and Valves
- Gas Piping
- Geometry
- Heating Systems
- Installation Practices
- National Fuel Gas Code
- National Plumbing Code
- Plumbing and Construction Basics
- Plumbing Essentials and Tools
- Plumbing Mathematics
- Plumbing Vents and Sewage Pumps
- Piping Materials and Joining Methods
- Science for Plumbing
- Service and Repair
- Surveying Instruments
- Water Heaters

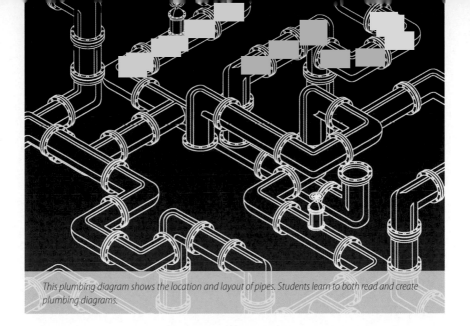
This plumbing diagram shows the location and layout of pipes. Students learn to both read and create plumbing diagrams.

Students in associate's degree programs take more advanced courses, such as water hydraulics, water distribution systems, and advanced piping.

You can combine practical training with course-based learning by choosing a school that offers a co-op program. In a co-op program, you work as an intern or apprentice part-time, while also taking academic courses. When a school arranges internships, students work in an unpaid position with a firm in the field. Because you experience the job firsthand, you can see if you are well suited for the physical and technical demands of the plumbing industry. It also helps you learn how plumbers interact with other contractors and their customers. In addition, an internship gives you a chance to make contacts in the industry. These contacts can be very helpful when you start looking for work, or they can provide you with a reference.

It is also possible to study plumbing through an online program. This approach lets you complete your coursework at your own pace at home, outside of working hours. This means you can work full-time while studying. Online training doesn't provide the same type of hands-on experience as a physical course, so you are reliant on the plumber for whom you are working to provide you with the practical experience needed. It is common for apprentice and journeyman plumbers to use online programs to complete the academic part of their training required for licensing because it allows them to work full-time while doing so.

If you do decide to enroll in an online program, it is important to make sure that the school you choose is accredited. Making sure the school is accredited ensures that your training will be acceptable to licensing authorities and that you can transfer credits you obtain from an online certificate course to another school, if you later decide to pursue a degree in plumbing technology. The US Department of Education maintains a database of accredited colleges that you can consult on their website.

Requirements for licensing differ from state to state, and you may be required to complete additional hands-on training to become licensed in certain states. Make sure to research your state's licensing requirements before committing to a specific plumbing training program.

Apprenticeship

It takes four to five years of apprenticeship to become a plumber. One way to obtain an apprenticeship is to apply for one through a labor union. This type of apprenticeship will allow you to become a member of the union, which can be beneficial if you want to work on construction projects in some locations or specialties, such as public works. Another way to become an apprentice is to arrange to work for a plumbing contractor or company. Apprentices are paid while training, although their salary is lower than that of journeymen and master plumbers.

Licensing

Plumbers must have a license to work in the field. The National Plumbing Code sets out the rules and regulations followed by all plumbers. However, there is no national licensing process for plumbers. Plumbers must be licensed by the state in which they work, and each state has particular requirements for academic and practical training. Some cities have their own regulations and licensing requirements, in addition to those of the state. As with other trades, most states recognize three basic levels of plumbers: apprentice, journeyman, and master. However, some states have only two levels: apprentice and plumber.

It is important to make sure that your training complies with the requirements of the area in which you work. Therefore, you should find out the licensing requirements in your state before you start training. Most states require applicants to be at least eighteen years old. However, some states allow individuals to obtain an apprentice license at sixteen. In all cases, applicants must have a high school diploma or GED (General Educational Development, a high school equivalency certificate, often called a General Education Diploma), and pass math and English tests.

In most cases, to be granted a license, an individual must complete a certain number of years training under the supervision of a fully licensed plumber, then pass a test. Most states have different levels of licenses. A trainee or apprentice license allows a trainee or apprentice plumber to work under a licensed plumber to learn the trade. Apprentice licenses are only available to students who are in an apprenticeship program or working for a master plumber who agrees to supervise them and keep track of the apprentice's hours. Typically, trainee plumbers must work 2,000 hours and undergo at least 144 hours of academic training. Some states allow trainees to get all their training on the job.

Once a plumber completes an apprenticeship, he or she becomes a journeyman. Journeymen work for a master plumber, but they can work on projects independently. In contrast, once a plumber receives a master's license, he or she can work completely independently. Many states require master plumbers to take continuing education courses every year or so to keep their licenses. This ensures that their knowledge of plumbing regulations and technology is up to date. Continuing education courses can be taken either in person or online, and through professional organizations, colleges, or technical schools.

Journeymen Plumbers

After plumbers complete their apprenticeship and successfully obtain a license, they become journeymen. A person must meet the state requirements for years of experience or hours of work and complete the necessary coursework to qualify for a journeyman license. Not all states offer journeyman licenses for plumbers. Some have only two levels: apprentice and master.

By the time plumbers become journeymen, they have the academic and practical training to carry out projects independently. The exact number of years required to qualify as a journeyman varies from state to state, but in most cases it is at least five. In some states, fewer years of work experience may be required for those with a higher level of education. A journeyman can install pipes, pumps, drains, vents, water mains, plumbing fixtures, HVAC systems, and other plumbing components without supervision. Journeymen are often sent out on service calls on their own. In many states, a journeyman plumber can bid on jobs. A journeyman plumber can read blueprints, and, on a construction site, a journeyman performs independent tasks according to the plans laid out by the master plumber. Some states allow journeymen to independently perform jobs only under a certain dollar amount, such as $500; otherwise, they must be supervised by a master plumber. If a journeyman is working for a master plumber, the master plumber assigns projects to the journeyman and checks over his or her work. While working on a project, the journeyman can consult the master plumber about problems or issues he or she encounters.

Master Plumbers

A person is qualified to become a master plumber after working three to five years as a journeyman and completing formal education in plumbing, safety regulations, and plumbing codes. A journeyman plumber can take the courses necessary to qualify for the master

Plumbers install an industrial air conditioner. Heating, ventilation, and air conditioning (HVAC) is a plumbing specialty.

exam at a brick-and-mortar or online school. Many professional organizations in the industry offer these courses as well. To be licensed as a master plumber, a person must pass a master plumber licensing test.

A master plumber has completed all of his or her training and holds the highest-level license. Many master plumbers choose to start their own companies. However, some master plumbers prefer the security of working for a services company or a contractor. Master plumbers design plumbing projects for residential, commercial, and industrial construction. In some states, one must be a master plumber to obtain permits for the plumbing portion of construction work. When master plumbers undertake a project, they draw up the plans showing the layout of pipes, vents, and fixtures. The master plumber decides on the types of materials, pipes, and fixtures used in a plumbing system. If a company or project employs journeymen or apprentice plumbers, they operate under the supervision of a master plumber. The master plumber assigns journeymen and apprentices to specific tasks and oversees their work.

To become a master plumber, you must have a specified amount of work experience, based on years of service or hours of work. The exact amount required varies from state to state. In addition, you must complete required coursework in plumbing technology. The classes can be taken in vocational and technical schools, colleges, or programs run by a plumbers' union or professional plumbing trade associations, such as the American Society of Plumbing Engineers (ASPE). There also are a number of online educational resources. After becoming a master plumber, you will be required to take continuing education courses at regular intervals, usually annually, to keep your knowledge up to date.

Advanced Training

Some plumbers choose to obtain additional education so they can work in specialized fields of plumbing. Among these areas are heating, air conditioning, and ventilation equipment; steamfitting; hydraulic systems; and chemical processing systems. Becoming qualified in these areas may require additional coursework that covers procedures and processes specific to the specialty. This training teaches the plumber about the operation and installation of particular equipment used in the specialty; the components and materials required; and the safety procedures necessary to protect themselves and others.

Working as a Plumber

Once you are licensed as a master plumber, you have various options for employment. One option is to work for

Pipefitters weld pipes in a facility under construction. Pipefitters require specialized training.

a contractor; another is to work for a plumbing or HVAC company. When the company is owned by someone else, the owner is responsible for the business side of the organization. You will be paid a salary and usually receive benefits such as health insurance and paid vacation. You might work for a company that provides general plumbing services, such as ABC Plumbing and Heating Company, or a company that requires staff plumbers to install the systems it sells, like a company selling HVAC systems. Working for a company provides you with security. Your salary is guaranteed, regardless of variations in business, and you will usually receive some type of benefits. When you work for a company, you concentrate on the work you do on projects and do not have to worry about the financial and managerial responsibilities of running a business. There are, however, downsides to working for a company as opposed to working for yourself. You must do the projects you are assigned rather than having the freedom to choose what work you do or the projects you prefer. Also, you may have less control over your schedule. A company supervisor or scheduler may assign plumbers to jobs according to the customers who call or projects that need to be done. If you work for a company that specializes in a particular area of plumbing, you may do the same type of work over and over. On one hand, your salary is secure, but on the other, your earnings are limited to the amount of your salary. You cannot increase the amount you earn, as an independent contractor can, by taking on more customers or larger projects.

Working for Yourself

Many plumbers choose to work as independent contractors. An independent contractor must find his or her own clients and do the work required to land jobs. As an independent contractor, you can apply for projects that interest you. If you prefer residential work or industrial work, you can limit yourself to a specialty. Independent contractors must advertise their services to find customers. Frequently, they advertise in the yellow pages, in local giveaway flyers, and/or through online websites such as HomeAdvisor.com or Angie's List. Others apply for plumbing jobs on large construction projects.

Joining a Union

Many plumbers and pipefitters choose to join labor unions. Labor unions are organizations that represent workers in a specific trade or group of related trades. There are labor unions that represent different types of tradespeople involved in the construction industry. The unions available for plumbers vary from place to place.

STARTING YOUR OWN BUSINESS

One option for master plumbers is to start their own business. Working for yourself gives you more freedom than working for someone else's company, but it also places all the financial and administrative burdens of running the company on your shoulders. As a master plumber, you should have the technical know-how to perform plumbing work. However, when you own a business, you also have to handle budgeting, accounting, inventory, and human resources. A plumbing company usually

A plumber fixes a sink. Many plumbers who perform repairs in residential construction operate their own businesses.

requires at least one administrative employee to answer the phone, make appointments, order supplies, and perform similar activities. If your company installs plumbing systems on construction projects, you will need to create plumbing plans, apply for permits for the plumbing work, and draft plumbing construction drawings. If your business is successful, you may decide to hire other plumbers. Among these employees may be journeymen and apprentices, who need to be supervised and trained. When you work for yourself, your earnings are limited only by how much business you bring in. This can be both an advantage and a disadvantage. If you are good at finding customers and projects, you can earn more. But if times are hard or you are not good at marketing, you may earn less than you would by working for someone else.

If you choose to start a business, it is important to make sure you have an adequate understanding of the financial and managerial responsibilities of running a company. If you are not knowledgeable in this area, you should take some courses in finance, human resources management, marketing, and accounting, at a local community college, at night school, or online.

You can find one in your area by doing an Internet search for "plumbers union" followed by the name of your city or state. Union members elect representatives, who negotiate salary and benefits with employers on behalf of the members. This process is called "collective bargaining" and results in a contract that spells out the terms of employment and the responsibilities of employers and workers. To provide funds for union operations, members pay monthly dues, which are usually automatically taken off their paycheck and sent to the union.

There are a number of benefits to union membership. While some areas have instituted "right-to-work" laws, which allow builders to hire nonunion as well as union workers, many cities and states require builders to hire union labor for major construction projects. Therefore, membership may provide better access to work. In some cases, union workers earn better pay than individual contractors, because the union has a large membership and therefore more power to negotiate than a single person. Employers of union workers may also be required to provide benefits not given to individual contractors. Unions also provide employment protection to workers and provide better job security. For example, an employer can fire a nonunion individual contractor at any time for any reason. However, he or she can only fire a union member for very specific reasons. In addition, unions maintain a list of projects for which workers are needed, which provides a resource for those looking for jobs. Because unions operate on a seniority system, those who have been members longest have priority when jobs or promotion opportunities come up. This is good if you have been a member for a long time but may limit opportunities for new members, who may find it hard to get work if the economy is in a downturn and jobs are scarce.

There are negatives to working for a union as well. Union members give up their independence and agree to go along with the decisions the union makes. At times when union representatives cannot reach an agreement with an employer, the union may call for a strike. This means that members of the union refuse to work and often form picket lines to gain public support for their cause. If the strike goes on for a long time, union members can suffer financial hardship because they are not earning money. Some unions maintain benevolent funds, which can be used to help members in case of hardship or emergencies. Factors that may affect your decision whether or not to join a union will depend on how powerful unions are in the construction industry in your area and the availability of nonunion apprenticeship opportunities.

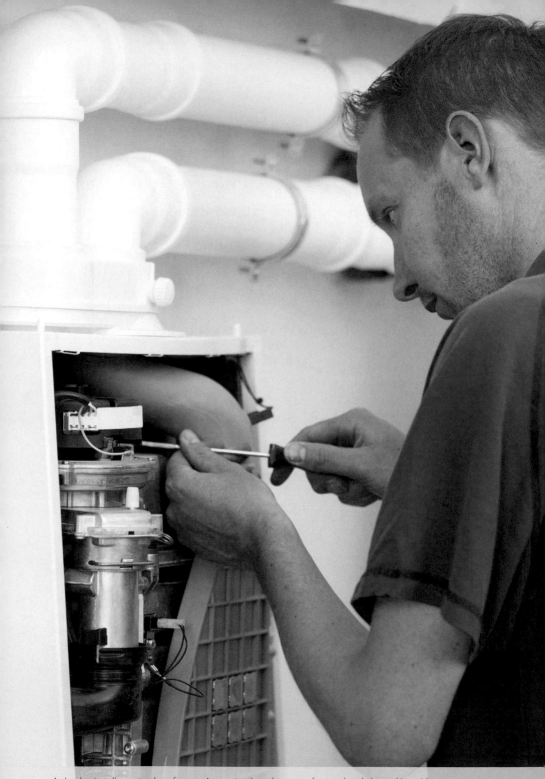

A plumber installs a natural gas furnace. Apprentices learn how to perform such tasks by working with journeymen plumbers.

CHAPTER 3

On the Job

What is it really like to be a plumber? What do plumbers do on a daily basis, and what are the typical activities of the different specialty plumbing professions?

Working as an Apprentice Plumber

An apprentice plumber works at least forty to fifty hours a week. During work hours, the apprentice works alongside a journeyman plumber, who teaches him or her how to perform different types of tasks. How much of the actual work an apprentice does on each job depends on what the journeyman plumber thinks he or she can handle. On a construction job, apprentices are primarily there to observe and learn. On a given job they carry materials, hold objects while the plumber connects

A residential plumber installs a sink. Residential plumbers often install new fixtures and pipes.

them, help install fixtures, and place pipe. Apprentices also watch the experienced plumbers interacting with customers. Thus, they learn how to handle customer relations as well as perform technical tasks. Apprentices also perform cleanup duty. After work, they might attend training classes several days a week.

Working as a Journeyman

Journeymen are assigned work by a master plumber. They may be sent on calls for residential or commercial work, or work on systems being installed in new construction. On a construction project, journeymen are assigned to work independently on specific tasks. They might, for instance, install pipes, fixtures, and appliances, or plumb heating, cooling, and sprinkler systems.

When working as a journeyman, it is important to get along with your fellow contractors. Developing good working relationships with other workers can help you secure opportunities to work together on future projects. You earn the respect of other contractors by demonstrating reliability, cooperating with others, and doing outstanding work.

A journeyman plumber will typically work eight hours or more during the day. In order to advance to master plumber, he or she will have to spend another two to three hours after work taking classes several days a week.

Working as a Residential Plumber

A plumber's day starts early in the morning. A plumber on call must be ready to handle emergencies outside of normal working hours. If a person's dishwasher is not working, he or she can wait till normal business hours for a service call, but if the kitchen is flooding, that's not possible. A plumber may have to get up at 5 a.m. to deal with a plumbing emergency. If a plumbing services company has multiple plumbers, they will most likely take turns being on call. If a plumber is self-employed, he or she will have to handle emergencies alone.

Assuming there are no early morning emergencies, a plumber's day typically starts around 7 or 8 a.m. If the plumber is an independent contractor, he or she will need to check to see if any customers have called. If there are new appointments that need to be made, he or she will have to fit them into the existing schedule. Sometimes customers have urgent problems that need to be handled the same day. Other customers may have requests that can be addressed at a later date, such as a request for a quote on updating pipes or installing a new sink or toilet. Sometimes there will be materials or parts that must be ordered as the result of the previous day's appointments. At either the beginning or the end of the day, the plumber will need to deal with administrative work, such as updating customer records on the computer, sending out invoices, or filling out sales tax forms. A larger plumbing company may have office staff who handle this type of work. Once the plumber has dealt with the early morning tasks, he or she loads up a van with the tools and parts required for that day's appointments and drives to the first job of the day. The plumber will do many different types of work, such as installing new pipes or fixtures in some locations, and solving problems at others to figure out why drains, toilets, sinks, or pipes are not working correctly. If a kitchen or bathroom in a home is being renovated, the plumber may need to install new pipes, a tub, a shower, and/or a sink, as well as any hardware required, such as faucets, showerheads, and drains. He or she may also need to install vent pipes that exit through the roof.

The plumber may have to climb through a narrow hatch into an attic, with materials and tools, and then balance on the ceiling joists to install heating or air-conditioning equipment or vent pipes. The actual installation of vents and pipes that run along the ceiling may require standing on a ladder while working. At another call, the plumber may be asked to replace fixtures such as toilets and sinks. This requires him or her to disconnect and remove the old fixture, locate the pipes, and attach a new fixture to them. When he or she is done, the plumber must clean up any debris from the work. After finishing the jobs, he or she drives back to the office and turns in copies of the paperwork written on the job, showing the charges and quotes given to customers. This information will be entered into the company's accounting and quote-tracking systems. Leaving the company's van, the plumber takes his or her own car home. After dinner, a plumber might use the computer to access a licensing preparation course over the Internet in order to study for his or her master plumber's licensing exam.

A plumber might get a call that someone has a problem whose cause is not immediately obvious. He or she will have to check the common reasons for the problem. Is there no water because of a break in a pipe or a clog, and if so, where? The plumber will ask questions such as "Has the problem happened before?" He or she will check for possible sources of the problem systematically. This may mean crawling through a crawlspace under the house to check the pipes. If the plumber finds a broken pipe, he or she can replace it, perhaps working in the tight space, using a flashlight to see. If the plumber cannot locate the problem, he or she may need to do an inspection of the interior of the pipes, using a camera on a flexible cable that can be fed into the pipes to inspect them from the inside. When the plumber finds the source break, he or she must remove the damaged section and replace it. This will require him or her to attach the new segment of pipe to the existing ones.

Working on Construction Projects

On residential construction jobs, plumbers install pipes and fixtures in single-family and multifamily homes. A construction project might consist of a single house or a number of houses, if the general contractor is building an entire housing development. The plumber will have to install, cut, and attach pipes throughout the house before the walls are closed up. He or she will have to attach the supply and waste pipes inside the house to the city water supply and the sewage pipes outside. If the house is on a concrete foundation, the pipes will need to be placed before the concrete is poured. The plumber may also have to install plumbing for exterior devices such as hot tubs, and water lines for outdoor spigots and sprinkler systems. In new construction, when placing pipes during rough-in, there will be no walls yet, so the plumber will be exposed to all kinds of weather. If the building is multistory, he or she may have to work on unfinished upper stories.

When working on a construction project, a plumber must review the blueprints and specifications, then assemble the necessary pipes, fixtures, and other components. Putting pipes in place is hard, heavy work. Pipes carrying water are made of copper, galvanized steel, or PVC. For a construction project, the plumber has to load his or her van with the necessary equipment and material, then drive to the work site. On larger construction projects, the plumber might arrange to have the pipes delivered directly to the site by the supplier. Depending on how much plumbing work needs to be done, he or she may have to work on the site for multiple days. Plumbing work on large construction projects such as office buildings or apartments may take place over days, weeks, or even months.

At the jobsite, the plumber must carry the pipes to the areas where they will be installed. Installing the pipes may require the plumber to work in cramped spaces. He or she cuts the pipes, and then connects them by gluing, soldering, or **threading**. When the plumber is finished for the day, he or she must clean up any debris and load tools and ladders into the van before leaving.

After the walls and ceiling are in place, the plumber will have to do finish work. He or she will install various types of appliances such as a refrigerator with an ice maker, a garbage disposal, a dishwasher, a hot-water heater, toilets, tubs, showers, and sinks. He or she may have to carry some of the appliances from the contractor's storage area to the location where they need to be installed.

When working on new buildings under construction, plumbers and pipefitters may be exposed to extreme temperatures, because the building is incomplete. Even if plumbing work is done at rough-in just before the walls are closed up, the plumber will need to work outdoors to connect pipes to city water and waste lines and to plumb outdoor pipes if they are required for externally located HVAC or sprinkler systems.

Working on a construction site can be demanding. There will be many types of contractors working at the same time, including roofers, carpenters, and electricians. It is necessary to work without getting in each other's way, and to make sure that work is coordinated so that no one is delayed in completing their portion of the job. Plumbers working on construction sites need to dress appropriately, wearing a hardhat and heavy boots for protection. There will be debris from construction work, and ruts from construction vehicles, on the ground. When installing plumbing fixtures and pipes inside a building, plumbers may have to contend with dust from plastering or sanding or fumes from painting.

Working as an Industrial Plumber

In-house and independent industrial plumbers perform work at manufacturing plants, water treatment plants, mines, foundries, and sewage treatment plants. At industrial plants, industrial plumbers read building plans and schematics to become familiar with the location and layout of the piping systems and components. They install supports and hangers for pipes, equipment, and fixtures. They install, maintain, and repair water treatment equipment, pipes, and controls; water heaters and piping; and plumbing fixtures. Industrial plumbers also install, maintain, and repair underground sanitation piping systems. In the course of their work, they must also perform routine maintenance. This requires testing piping systems to make sure that they are leak-free and, in the case of high-pressure pipes, that the pressure is at the correct level. If pipes need to be replaced, plumbers must make sure that any new pieces meet the required specifications and are properly installed. They must ensure that existing and new piping systems and components comply with all codes and environmental regulations. In-house plumbers at facilities such as water distribution or waste treatment plants may also be required to prepare

Industrial facilities, such as oil refineries and chemical processing plants, rely on industrial plumbers and pipefitters to install and repair complex piping systems.

budgets, order supplies, write reports, and coordinate work with other construction professionals.

Factories often contain pipes that carry water, oil, gas, steam, or chemicals used in industrial processes. When a plumbing problem develops in a factory, this may mean that processing must stop, which may result in financial loss for the company. In the case of a municipal water or power facility, plumbing problems may cause the loss of services to customers. Problems with high-pressure pipes or those carrying chemicals could result in injury to workers. In rare cases, if a problem is not addressed rapidly, a chemical spill or explosion may endanger people in the community. Therefore, if a plant has a problem with the pipes that supply water or other liquids or gases, the problem must be fixed immediately. Many manufacturing plants and processing facilities run at night, employing two or three shifts of workers. This means that if a problem occurs at night, an industrial plumber will need to respond.

Working as a Pipefitter

On commercial and industrial projects, pipefitters must install the pipes that bring water into and remove waste from office buildings, hospitals, schools, sports stadiums, and other large facilities. They must install the pipes

Working as a Pipeline Pipefitter

Long-distance pipelines are used to carry gasoline, crude oil, diesel and jet fuel, natural gas, and propane across the country in every direction. Utility companies, **refineries**, oil and gas companies, offshore drilling rigs, and contractors who specialize in building pipelines employ pipefitters to construct the pipes for these lines. There are more than one million miles (1.6 million km) of pipeline in the United States. Pipeline

A pipeline pipefitter working outdoors welds two segments of pipe together.

construction projects can cover hundreds of miles. However, there are also shorter links that need to be built, to connect a storage facility to a distribution center.

Today, most pipelines run underground. Work on a pipeline begins with a crew that clears and grades the area where a pipeline is to be laid. This is followed by the **excavation** of a ditch by a ditching crew using heavy equipment. Then, the pipefitters go to work. Steel pipe is strung alongside the ditch. Pipefitters use a bending machine to make the pipe match the **contours** of the **terrain** and go in the correct direction. The pipe is then welded into one long pipeline. Manual, semiautomatic, and/or automatic welding equipment might be used in the process. X-ray or **ultrasound** equipment is then used to ensure that the welds are all up to spec. The pipe is then lowered into the ditch, and the ditch is backfilled with the dirt that was removed from it using specialized construction vehicles and equipment that protect the pipe. Water is then run through the pipeline to make sure it operates at the correct pressure without leaking. If so, the pipeline is ready to use.

Pipeline pipefitters must be able to read pipeline flow and alignment diagrams. In addition to laying pipe, they maintain and perform repairs on it and on related devices and equipment as necessary. Being a pipeline pipefitter requires strength, stamina, and tolerance for working outdoors in adverse weather conditions.

that feed boilers and carry hot water or steam for heat throughout the building. In factories or processing plants that require pipes to carry liquids or gases, they must install high-pressure piping. High-pressure pipes are made of carbon steel, stainless steel, or a metal **alloy**. Pipefitters must cut the pipe precisely, then use threading, grooving, bending, and welding to connect the pieces.

Pipelayers

Pipelayers are different from pipefitters. Pipelayers assemble, connect, and construct pipe systems for storm or sanitation sewers, drains, and water mains. Pipelayers drive backhoes and trenching vehicles, which dig the trenches for the placement of sanitary sewer pipes and stormwater sewer drainpipes. They use surveyors' equipment to ensure that the trenches have the proper slope according to plans and specifications; they calculate and adjust the grade of the ground, using a level and laser. They then install lengths of pipe in the trenches. They measure and mark pipes for cutting and threading; cut, thread, hammer, and weld pipe using **pipe threaders** and benders; and connect the pipes by either gluing the segments together, attaching them with cement, or welding them. They secure the pipes with clamps, brackets, and hangers, then seal the joints. They attach

Pipelayers place an earthquake-resistant water pipe in a trench. The pipe is 20 feet (6.1 meters) long and weighs 1,000 pounds (453.6 kilograms).

the pipes to the sewer system by means of a valve, called a tap, and then cover them up. Pipelayers also inspect pipes and test them, using **hydrostatic** testing and other methods. To repair pipes, they must dig or excavate existing pipes.

Working as a Plumbing Foreman

The boss of a team of plumbers on a construction project is called a plumbing foreman. A plumbing foreman can be a journeyman or master plumber, but either way, he or she must have extensive experience installing plumbing on construction projects. The foreman reviews the work that is required then assembles a crew of plumbers to execute it.

Where the plumbing foreman gets his or her workers depends on whether it is a union or nonunion project.

If it is a union project, the foreman assembles the crew according to the union's hiring procedures. Generally, the union has a central location where it maintains a list of projects and assigns workers. Plumbers who are looking for work contact the union office. When an employer contacts the union with a project, plumbers on that list are contacted. Union members are not required to accept a job, but they are offered it in the order in which they signed up. They are more likely to accept a job if they respect the foreman. Foremen on union projects must be adept at working with people because the plumbers in the crew are assigned according to union rules, not chosen by the foreman. A foreman on a nonunion project is free to hire plumbers with whom he or she has worked previously or who have been recommended. However, they too are more likely to agree to work for the foreman if they respect him or her.

A plumbing foreman supervises the installation of all plumbing systems and their related devices and components, as well as all distilled and demineralized water distribution systems; fire protection systems; safety shower and eyewash systems; lawn sprinkler systems; acid waste and **dilution basins**; and water main, subsoil drainage, and distribution systems, in accordance with codes and regulations. The foreman assigns plumbers to tasks and coordinates their activities with those of other tradespeople working on the project. The foreman inspects the work site to determine methods of installation, and the types of pipe and material required. He or she assigns plumbers to specific tasks and supervises these activities. He or she also resolves any problems in layout, fabrication, and assembly encountered by plumbers working on the job. The foreman orders materials, including the tools necessary to complete the work.

Crew members rely on their foremen to make sure that they have high-quality tools, material, and equipment. The foreman must ensure that his or her crew has everything they need, ready when they need it. One of the foreman's most important responsibilities is supervising the plumbers and inspecting their work. To successfully manage a crew, a plumbing foreman must be fair, knowledgeable, and able to deal with problems efficiently. The success of a project depends on the ability of the foreman to assemble a team that can work well together and provide technical and personal leadership.

The Dangers of the Job

Safety is always a concern for plumbers. There are a number of ways that a plumber can be injured on the job. One of the most obvious aspects of working as a plumber is the need to take precautions when handling waste and other contaminants. Plumbers who work in commercial and industrial applications may be working with pipes that carry chemicals or acids. Nor are pipes the only source of contamination. Basements may have rodent droppings; facilities like hospitals can have pipes in areas that contain biohazardous material. Another common source of contamination is mold, which tends to grow in damp areas. It often occurs in bathrooms, under sinks, and in damp cellars. Many molds cause allergic reactions such as itchy eyes and throat and nose irritation. Some types of mold are even toxic. Therefore, it's important for plumbers to take precautions to protect themselves when working. First, they need to consider what types of contamination might be present in the area where they are working. They need to wear gloves, goggles, and respiratory masks, and long sleeves and long pants when working in areas with hazardous materials or mold. After work it is important to shower thoroughly and wash any contaminated clothing. If a home has a serious mold problem, the homeowner should be informed of this, so the necessary steps can be taken to remedy the problem.

Often pipes are located close to electrical wiring and gas lines and fixtures. Plumbers must be careful when working around these items to avoid starting a fire, especially when working with tools that could generate sparks on contact, or with welding or soldering equipment. It is also important to be aware of electrical wires and connections to avoid a shock. Shocks from low-voltage wiring are rarely fatal, but they hurt. Touching a metal pipe with one hand and an electrical contact accidentally with the other is unpleasant.

Plumbers have to stand on roof joists when working in the attic, and stand on ladders. Water can make a work area slippery. Therefore, there is always the danger of slipping and falling. Learning to fall safely (for example, head up, palms out, with your body folded) can help you avoid getting seriously hurt. Carrying heavy pipes and equipment can take a toll on your body, especially your back, shoulders, wrists, and knees. You can reduce wear and tear by learning and applying proper lifting techniques and using equipment such as lifting straps and dollies.

As with any job requiring tools and equipment, these need to be used carefully. Plumbers experience the usual injuries from hand tools such as hammers and cutting devices. When using automated machinery, they have to take care to avoid getting clothing, fingers, or hair caught in moving parts. In the course of plumbing work, flying particles and small objects, sparks, and chemicals can get in a plumber's eyes. Also, pipes can break and

Plumbers install pipes in a crawlspace. They wear sound-damping earmuffs to protect their ears from the noise of the equipment.

spray water or steam. Therefore, you should always wear eye protection, such as goggles, when working. You should also wear earplugs to protect your ears, if you are using loud, automated equipment. Taking appropriate precautions when working helps ensure that you have a long and productive career.

Pros and Cons of a Plumbing Career

Being a plumber provides the satisfaction of performing a service that helps people. If you like to build things, doing remodeling or new construction of bathrooms and kitchens can be gratifying work. If you work on large industrial projects or pipelines, there can be a great deal of **camaraderie** among workers, and you may have the opportunity to see interesting parts of the country. Among the advantages of being a plumber is having a constant variety of new activities to do and different problems to solve, and because of the range of plumbing jobs, you can work in different types of jobs. In addition, the salaries and hourly pay rates of fully qualified plumbers are good, so you can make a comfortable living.

One of the cons of working as a plumber is that the job is very physically demanding. You will have to lift and carry heavy pipes and equipment, climb ladders, and crawl through tight spaces. Also, the hours can be long and/or unpredictable. Plumbing emergencies can happen at any time, and dealing with them can't wait. If you work for yourself, either as an independent contractor on construction projects or running your own business, you have to market yourself, making contacts or finding customers.

New water **conservation** technologies and plumbing materials and equipment are constantly being developed, and existing equipment is constantly evolving, as new and improved versions replace older ones. This means that you must make a commitment to constantly update your skills and knowledge. However, being a plumber can be a satisfying and rewarding long-term career.

A plumber installs fixtures in a new house. Low-water usage fixtures can benefit both the homeowner and the environment.

CHAPTER 4

The Industry: Present and Future

According to the November–December issue of *Plumbing Perspective* magazine, an increase in residential construction and the continuing demand for remodeling projects equals a higher demand for plumbing, heating, and HVAC contractors around the country. Demand also continues to be high for "technology upgrades to energy-efficient HVAC and water-conserving plumbing systems." This area is likely to grow in demand because of two factors: an increasing interest in the use of technologies that are better for the environment, and the desire of consumers to reduce their costs for water and HVAC.

In 2008, a financial crisis occurred that caused a downturn in the economy. A wave of home foreclosures followed. Banks tightened their requirements for mortgages, and there was a decrease in the number of homes sold. In the wake of the crisis, companies in the home-building industry significantly reduced the number of houses they built, which has resulted in a shortage of new houses. Because people have had difficulty getting mortgages to buy a house, there has been a growing demand for apartments to rent. Increasing rents have

The demand for new homes and apartments is likely to create opportunities for plumbers who want to work on residential projects.

created continuing interest in constructing apartment buildings. These two factors are creating a boom in new residential construction. David Crowe, chief economist of the National Association of Home Builders (NAHB), has stated that steady job and economic growth will allow more people who have delayed home purchases to buy homes, and allow those looking to upgrade to larger homes to do so. The NAHB expects the number of new homes built to increase by 26 percent to 802,000 in 2015 and to reach 1.1 million units in 2016. The rental market has been a hot area since the economic crisis of 2008. Construction of multifamily housing is expected to continue on an upswing. For plumbers who work in the residential industry, it makes little difference whether people own or rent their homes or apartments. Plumbing systems are still required. As the economy continues to pick up, construction of new commercial and industrial facilities is also likely to increase. All of this bodes well for the employment of plumbers.

The NAHB Remodeling Index, which measures the amount of remodeling activity, reached an all-time high in the third quarter of 2014. The NAHB expects remodeling activity to grow 2.7 percent in 2015 and 1.3 percent in 2016. Better yet, according to the US Bureau of Labor Statistic's *Occupational Outlook Handbook*, the demand for plumbers is expected to increase at an annual rate of 21 percent, which is faster than the estimated growth rate for all jobs.

The median salary for plumbers is around $49,000, or about $23.50 an hour. However, pay varies widely, depending on the level of the plumbing professional. Apprentice plumbers generally earn 30 to 50 percent of what experienced plumber make. Plumbers in specialty areas earn higher salaries. Boilermakers, who assemble, install, and repair boilers and other large vessels that hold liquids and gases, make around $56,560, or $27 an hour. Industrial pipefitters, who install, repair, and maintain pipes for chemicals, acids, and gas, earn a median pay of approximately $58,000. The salary range for plumbers and pipefitters of all types is $45,000 to $84,000. For plumbers who own their businesses, wages can be even higher. The pay rates of union plumbers are sometimes higher than those of nonunion plumbers, but they must pay monthly union dues from their salary, which reduces their take-home pay.

The pay for plumbers, steamfitters, and pipefitters who are willing to work on projects overseas, such as energy **infrastructure** projects, is often even greater. Given the political unrest and attitudes toward Americans in some parts of the world, such work could involve personal safety risks. However, working overseas can also provide unique cultural and work experiences.

The population is aging, and the baby boomers, people born in the 1950s and 1960s, are retiring. The retirement of older plumbers provides opportunities for journeymen to move into more responsible positions. It also creates vacancies that can be filled by new apprentices.

Benefits

When you work for a company, you usually receive benefits as well as a salary. The exact benefits offered vary from company to company. Usually, large companies provide more benefits than small ones. Benefits might include paid vacation, health insurance, and tuition reimbursement for job-related schooling. Some companies offer additional types of insurance, such as life and disability. Large companies may give employees the chance to participate in 401(k) retirement plans. In this type of plan, employees put aside a portion of their pay for retirement, which they can invest in a variety of ways. Sometimes the company matches a small portion of the employee's contribution. Union workers receive a variety of benefits through the union; representatives of the union negotiate for benefits with employers, and all union members receive the same benefits. If a plumber is self-employed, he or she must make sure to obtain adequate insurance coverage, including health and disability insurance, and possibly life insurance.

Getting a Job

When the time comes to look for a plumbing job, you need to begin by making a decision about the environment in which you want to work and the type of work you want to do. Do you want to apply for a union apprenticeship and work your way up through the ranks? This may be a good choice if you are interested in working on large construction projects. If you want to concentrate on residential or industrial work, you may prefer the nonunion approach. In this case, you will need to find a job working for an established plumber or plumbing services company. Depending on the part of the country in which you work, construction work may be seasonal, but residential and industrial work will occur year-round. The decision whether or not to join a union will also be influenced by where you choose to work. In some states and highly populated urban areas, construction work is heavily unionized. In other places, jobs are available for both union and nonunion tradespeople. Some areas even have "right-to-work" laws, which prohibit employers from discriminating against nonunion workers.

If you are interested in becoming a union plumber, you will need to contact your local plumbing union. You can search online for plumbers' unions in your city or state. Contact the union for information on applying for an apprentice position. The best time to look for union apprenticeships is in the spring, when most new construction projects are getting underway.

There are a variety of ways to find nonunion apprentice positions. The most common way to look for jobs today is to check out online job-hunting sites such as CareerBuilder. com. Search for "plumber apprentice" or "pipefitter" to obtain a list of companies looking for entry-level plumbing employees. It's common today for companies, including utilities, to have a "Jobs" or "Careers" section on their website to advertise positions they are trying to fill. You can also check out the want ads in the employment section of your local paper, either in the print edition or online. Many people are likely to respond to advertised positions. To maximize your chances of finding a job, you may want to compile a list of plumbers and plumbing companies in your area and send them a cover letter and résumé. The cover letter should state that you are looking for an apprentice position. Even if a position is not immediately available, many employers keep résumés on file and may contact you if a position becomes available.

Companies in areas that rely on piping systems for their production, such as chemical-processing and oil-refining companies, may hire in-house plumbers, steamfitters, gasfitters, or pipefitters, as do municipal water supply, waste management, and public works organizations.

Another way to find out about plumbing jobs is to attend a job fair, an event where local and/or national companies send representatives to a school or community site to find employees. At a job fair you can ask representatives about jobs available for plumbers or pipefitters. This is especially true of companies in the energy, chemical processing, and utility industries. The company representative can tell you whom to contact at the company and also provide you with general information about the company.

Your school can also be a job-hunting resource. Often vocational schools have established relationships and contacts with businesses in the community, and they may help you with job hunting. If you go on to study at a community college or online course after high school, check to see if they provide placement assistance. Many schools provide job-hunting assistance to graduates.

If your school includes practical work as part of its vocational program, keep a record of the contact information for everyone in the field you work with or meet. Networking is one of the best ways to find work.

When you are looking for a job, you can call people on your contact list. Even if they don't have a job opening, they can recommend other people to contact. In addition, if they hear that someone is looking to hire, they can let that person know you are looking for work, or pass the information along to you. For the same reason, while you are in school, consider joining a student chapter of an organization such as the National Association of Homebuilders. Participating in a professional organization gives you the chance to learn about the trade, and you can meet professionals who can become valuable contacts when you are looking for work. Once you have a job, they can also provide you with advice and answer any career-related questions you may have.

Preparing a Résumé

Your best tool for gaining potential employers' interest is your résumé. A résumé informs employers about your training and experience to highlight why you would be a good candidate for the job. There are many formats for résumés; however, when looking for an entry-level job, you don't want to use a complicated format. Keep your résumé simple and easy to understand. It should be well-organized and professional-looking. You should include your name, address, phone number, and e-mail address at the top. The résumé should start with a statement of the position you are applying for. If you are responding to an ad, refer to that job posting. If you are not, indicate that you are seeking a plumbing apprentice position.

The next section covers your work experience. You should include all the jobs you've worked at, including work/study, part-time, and summer jobs. If you haven't worked at jobs relating to construction or plumbing, emphasize aspects of your work experience that indicate that you have the qualities to be a good apprentice. These might include working outside of normal hours, providing good customer service, coming up with useful ideas, solving problems, and the like.

In the next section, provide information about your education and training. This should include any vocational training. If you haven't taken a vocational course, you'll want to include relevant courses you've taken, such as science, math, computer, and shop classes. In the final section, provide other information that might be relevant, such as the fact that you speak a second language.

Your résumé represents the quality of the work you do. Employers want employees who are careful, thorough, neat, and detail-oriented. Therefore, you want your résumé to reflect those qualities. Make sure to proofread your résumé and fix any typos or grammatical mistakes. It's a good idea to have another person read it as well. Don't just use a spell checker. It can miss simple mistakes such as absent words or places where a word is spelled right but is incorrect (for example, "hole" instead of "whole").

Job Interviews

The next stage of job hunting is the interview. This is your chance to convince a potential employer that you are the best person for the job. Before you go to the interview, you can look up information about the company on the Internet. That way you can talk to the interviewer specifically about the company and why you would be a good fit. The first impression you make when an employer sees you will have a great influence on him or her. Therefore, you need to present yourself in a way that assures an employer that you are professional. The first aspect of presenting yourself well is dressing in neat, clean, work-appropriate clothing. This might consist of slacks and a shirt for a man or a skirt and a blouse or pantsuit for a woman. Even though you might wear work clothes on a job, these are not appropriate for an interview.

How you speak during an interview is significant as well. An employer will judge how you are likely to talk to customers from how you speak at the interview, so be sure to use proper grammar and speak respectfully and clearly.

The interviewer will most likely ask you two types of questions. Of course, he or she will want to know about your work and educational experience. These are factual questions. He or she won't expect you to have a deep knowledge of plumbing because you are applying for an apprentice position. However, the interviewer will want to know you are capable of learning the material and handling the physical aspects of the job. Therefore, be prepared to give examples that show you have the qualities the employer is looking for. If you have completed a vocational program, you should be able to answer questions that show your basic knowledge of plumbing. It's also common for interviewers to ask questions designed to establish how you approach solving problems and how you handle stress. Faced with this kind of question, be prepared to respond with the steps you would take to address the situation. It is not necessary to actually solve the problem. The employer is trying to assess how you think and handle yourself.

Moving Forward

One option for a master plumber is to open his or her own business. Those who choose to do this can earn high incomes. Their success is limited only by how they grow the business, taking on more customers and larger projects. This is not the only option for advancement, however.

A full-time employee of a utility company, waterworks company, sewage treatment facility, hospital, university, or industrial plant can move up to a management position. He or she might become a plumbing foreman or building supervisor, or a facility supervisor or manager in the case of multibuilding facilities such as university or industrial campuses. Managers in these areas have the same responsibilities as managers in any business. They hire, fire, schedule, and supervise workers. They also perform inventory management, making sure the department has the correct type and amount of material, tools, and equipment. They must create and track budgets to make sure that the department's funds are used appropriately. Often, they must report to senior management on the state of the facilities and on requirements for new components or equipment. They may be part of an emergency response team, which deals with disasters that affect the water supply and piping systems in the facility. In this case, they have to draw up plans for responding to and dealing with emergencies.

One option for union plumbers is to move into union management. This involves obtaining a management position in the local chapter first, and then possibly advancing into management at the national level. Managers do not work as plumbers. Instead, they run

PROFESSIONAL ORGANIZATIONS

Joining a professional organization can have a number of advantages. It gives you access to printed and online resources. Through meetings and conferences, you have the opportunity to learn more about plumbing and the industry. Meetings also help you get to know professionals whom you can call for information or advice.

Some trade organizations have student chapters or resources. They may provide financial or practical help to minority or low-income students seeking to enter the field. Once you have a job, professional organizations can be a resource for licensing courses and continuing education necessary to stay up to date. The following are some trade organizations of interest to plumbers:

American Association of Sanitary Engineering (AASE)
The AASE provides certification, standards, and publications for plumbers involved in sanitary engineering.
www.asse-plumbing.org

American Society of Plumbing Engineers (ASPE)
The ASPE provides education, certification, and information for those in the plumbing industry.
www.aspe.org

American Subcontractors Association (ASA)
The ASA provides support and resources for tradespeople working on construction projects.
www.asaonline.com

American Water Works Association (AWWA)

The AWWA provides a wide range of educational resources, device-specific information, a career center, and publications for water professionals.

www.awwa.org

Coalition of Labor Union Women (CLUW)

America's only national organization for union women. CLUW's mission is to unify all union women to determine and address common problems and concerns.

www.cluw.org

National Association of Minority Contractors (NAMC)

The NAMC provides access, advocacy, and development for members, and has chapters around the country.

namcnational.org

National Kitchen and Bath Association (NKBA)

The NKBA offers a variety of publications, educational programs, and student webinars for those involved in the design and construction of kitchens and bathrooms.

www.nkba.org

Plumbing-Heating-Cooling Contractors Association (PHCC)

The PHCC offers a variety of tools for plumbing contractors, including information on running a business.

www.phccweb.org

the union, establish policies, and oversee union activities. They engage in activities such as organizing unions in nonunionized companies, negotiating with employers and government representatives, and allocating the financial resources of the union.

Large contractors often employ an estimator, a plumber whose work consists of calculating the time and cost of materials needed for projects. Estimators play a key role in large construction projects. They study project plans, then estimate the amount of time, workers, and materials

A supervisor at a water treatment plant studies water flow. One of his responsibilities is to ensure treated water meets purity specifications.

required. After these needs have been established, they create bid proposals. An estimator must ensure that their company makes an adequate profit, while not presenting a proposal that is so expensive that the company loses the bid.

A master plumber can choose to become a municipal plumbing inspector and work for the city. He or she issues permits to contractors for plumbing work, then inspects the work performed to make sure it complies with plumbing codes. Plumbing inspectors play an important role in ensuring that the plumbing systems in buildings are safe.

If you find you are interested in designing systems or inventing new devices, another option is to undertake additional education to become a plumbing systems engineer or civil engineer. In contrast to a plumber or pipefitter, who installs, tests, and repairs pipes and plumbing fixtures, a plumbing systems engineer designs plumbing and piping systems for commercial, industrial, and municipal use. Civil engineers design large construction projects such as dams, bridges, tunnels, and systems for water supply and waste treatment. They may also design large pipelines and industrial piping systems. Plumbing system and civil engineers may work in private industries or government facilities. They have at least a bachelor's degree in plumbing systems or civil engineering, and many go on to earn a master's degree or PhD in

A plumbing inspector performs an audit of a factory's plumbing systems to make sure they meet the plumbing code requirements.

civil engineering. Another option is to become a water quality scientist. Water scientists study various aspects of the water supply to make sure that it is safe and adequate. They study drinking water, surface water (lakes, rivers, and estuaries), and groundwater. They test water samples for bacterial or chemical contamination, investigate cases of water pollution, and provide advice for dealing with incidents of contamination or pollution. Water quality scientists generally have at least a bachelor's of science degree in chemistry, biochemistry, geology, or ecology.

What the Future Holds

There is likely to be a continued demand for energy-efficient HVAC systems and low-water-usage plumbing systems. In many areas, there are state and sometimes local incentives for homeowners and businesses that install such systems. This is especially likely in the western and southwestern states, which suffer from limited water supplies. Green plumbing is only going to grow in importance. Both homeowners and businesses are interested in using resources in a way that is ecologically sound. This is called sustainability. Sustainability in terms of plumbing requires using water as efficiently as possible and recycling it where possible.

Using water efficiently requires being familiar with and installing low-flow valves and fixtures. For industrial uses, there are approaches that save water, such as using high-pressure, low-volume nozzles on spray hoses. Industrial plumbers are likely to be called upon to conduct audits of facilities and to make recommendations about ways to reduce water usage and suggestions for more energy-efficient equipment, such as industrial refrigeration and hydraulic systems. Recycling water involves installing graywater systems. These systems are becoming increasingly common in industrial and commercial applications, and their use is likely to grow in residential applications as well. Graywater systems collect used water from non-waste applications such as showers, store it in a tank, and use it for non-drinking-water applications, such as watering plants.

Computer technology is changing the way that plumbing systems in buildings operate. In residential construction, applications exist that let homeowners remotely turn off plumbing fixtures such as faucets and control air-conditioning systems and appliances from a smartphone or tablet.

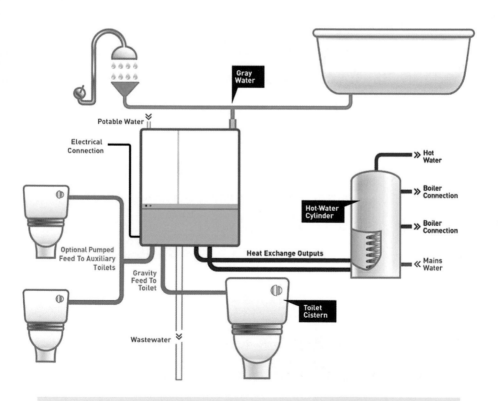

In this example of a graywater system, water is collected from the shower and bathtub and reused to flush toilets.

The trend toward computer automation is likely to continue in the future. Many new factories (and older factories that are being upgraded), processing plants, and water and waste treatment facilities are installing systems that are run and monitored almost solely by computers. These systems use sensors to send information to a computer to issue a warning if there is a problem with any part of the system. So, whether you work on new construction or fix systems in finished buildings, you will need to be familiar with how computers and computer-controlled systems operate, and how to interact with them when installing and repairing plumbing components, working with HVAC equipment, and piping buildings.

The Evolving Construction Industry

Contractors are using computer applications to design buildings as well as to control systems within them. One of the technologies that is being used increasingly in construction is **three-dimensional (3-D) rendering**. This type of application allows contractors and architects to create three-dimensional views of piping systems. The 3-D view is useful for seeing how components fit together across floors and in relation to other elements in the building. Virtual reality technology is another computer technology being developed in the construction industry.

This plumber is servicing an electronic system that controls hot water and heating.

It uses computers to allow a contractor to "walk around" a 3-D interior of a building and view the location of elements as if he or she were actually in the building.

Systems in a building are increasingly incorporating elements of more than one trade. For example, heating and cooling systems may be installed by plumbers but have electronic controls that are part of a larger system installed by electricians. In addition, computer-based monitoring systems are being used to keep track of the state of plumbed systems and fixtures throughout facilities. Plumbers are likely to find themselves recruited to work on teams of contractors that include other tradespeople such as electricians. They will need to work together on construction and renovation projects, especially those for large buildings or facilities. Instead of a general contractor obtaining quotes separately from subcontractors in different trades, subcontractors will use collaborative software on computers to arrive at a joint quote. Ecological considerations, the need for water conservation, and ever more advanced electronic applications are likely to continue to change the nature of plumbing over time. To be successful as a plumber, it will be necessary to adapt to these changes as they occur.

As you can see, being a plumber can be a demanding but satisfying profession. It can provide you with a good income, present interesting challenges, and also allow you to work with new technologies that promote sustainability and protect the environment. If you are willing to put in the time to master the craft of plumbing, it can provide you with a long, rewarding career.

Glossary

alloy A combination of two or more metals.

camaraderie A feeling of friendship and mutual support.

conservation Preserving an element such as water.

contour Shape.

dilution basin A pool where acids or chemicals are diluted with water to safe levels.

excavation The process of digging up; in the case of pipe, often done with a construction vehicle such as a backhoe.

galvanize To apply a zinc coating to steel or iron to make it more rust-resistant.

general contractor The head contractor on a job. He or she usually hires the other contractors.

hydrojetting Spraying high-pressure jets of water down pipes to clean them.

hydrostatic Using a fluid, such as water, that is not under pressure.

independent contractor A person who works for him- or herself rather than for a company.

infrastructure The basic systems serving a facility, city, or other area.

pipe threader A machine that creates thread in the ends of pipes.

potable Safe to drink; drinkable.

refinery A facility that converts a raw material, such as crude oil, into a finished product, such as gasoline.

subcontractor A contractor in a specialty such as electricity or plumbing hired by a general contractor.

terrain The surface and features of a piece of land.

thread In regard to pipe, spiral ridges on the interior or exterior of pipe that makes it possible to screw two pieces together.

three-dimensional (3-D) rendering Using special software and/or virtual reality devices to create a three-dimensional image of a building.

trap In plumbing, a curved or U-shaped pipe in which liquid sits to prevent gases from passing up or down the pipe.

ultrasound A type of imaging that uses sound waves bounced off an object, such as a pipe, to create a picture.

weld To heat the ends of two pieces of metal so that they will melt together using handheld, partially automated, or automated welding equipment.

Further Information

Books

Josh, Gregory. *Cool Careers: Plumbing.* North Mankato, MN: Cherry Lake Publishing, 2011.

Nixon, James. *What We Do: Plumbers.* London: Franklin Watts, 2014.

Payment, Simone. *Essential Careers: A Career as a Plumber.* New York: Rosen Publishing, 2010.

Websites

Explore the Trades
www.explorethetrades.org
This organization's website allows students to explore various aspects of a career in a trade, including being a plumber.

Plumber Pre-Apprentice Training
clearfield.jobcorps.gov/Libraries/pdf/plumbing.sflb
This site explains the training available for young people that prepares them for an entry-level job in the plumbing field.

United Association of Journeymen and Apprentices of the Plumbing and Pipefitting Industry of the United States and Canada.
www.helmetstohardhats.org/career-path/united-association-of-journeymen-and-apprentices-of-the-plumbing-and-pipe-fitting-industry-of-the-united-states-and-canada
This website provides information on apprenticeship and certification programs for plumbers.

Bibliography

Allgood Plumbing and Electric. "Technological Advances in Plumbing." Retrieved June 15, 2015. http://www.callallgood.com/blog/technological-advances-in-plumbing

Alliance for Water Efficiency. "Water Saving Tips: Commercial, Industrial, and Institutional Water Use." http://www.allianceforwaterefficiency.org/CII-tips.aspx.

Association for Union Democracy. "Hiring Hall Procedures in the Construction Trades," www.uniondemocracy.org/UDR/132-Hiring_Hall_Procedures_in_the_Construction_Trades.htm.

Clever Job Hunter. *How to Become a Plumber.* Amazon Digital Services, 2011.

Conick, Hal. "Top 10 Safety Hazards of Working as a Plumber." http://contractormag.com/plumbing/top-10-safety-hazards-working-plumber#slide-0-field_images-406131.

Contractor magazine. "A Day in the Life of a Plumbing Apprentice." http://contractormag.com/plumbing/cm_newsarticle_745.

DeMerceau, John. "Things You Can Do with a Journeyman's License." Chron.com. http://work.chron.com/things-can-journeymans-license-3746.html.

Diman Regional Vocational Technical High School. "Plumbing Program Overview." http://plumbing.dimanregional.org/modules/groups/integrated_home.phtml?&gid=1512610.

French, A. L. Dawn. *Careers: Plumber.* Santa Lucia: Double F Publishing House, 2014

Hamlin, Kristen. "Job Fair Questions Students Need to Be Prepared to Answer," http://work.chron.com/job-fair-questions-students-need-prepared-answer-11037.html.

Hankey, Roger. "Basic Plumbing Principles." http://www.hankeyandbrown.com/xSites/Inspectors/hankeyandbrown/Content/UploadedFiles/basic%20plumbing%20principles%20ASHI%20GLC%202011.pdf.

Ivey Engineering. "27 Historical Events That Shaped Modern Plumbing." http://www.iveyengineering.com/blog/historical-events-plumbing-systems.

Joyner, Jeffrey. "What Skills Do You Need to Be a Plumber?" http://work.chron.com/skills-need-plumber-3637.html.

New England Institute of Technology. "Plumbing Technology." http://www.neit.edu/Programs/Associate-Degree-Programs/Building-Technologies/Plumbing-Technology.

Northwest Territories Municipal and Community Affairs. "Job Description: Plumber." http://www.maca.gov.nt.ca/school/tools/JD_docs/Plumber%20JD.pdf.

Penn Foster Career School. "Plumbing Training Program." http://www.pennfoster.edu/programs-and-degrees/construction-and-maintenance/plumber-career-diploma.

Plumbing and Mechanical Magazine. "The History of Plumbing: Roman and English Legacy." July 1989. http://www.theplumber.com/eng.html.

Plumbing Perspective. "Construction Outlook Is Positive for 2015: A Good Trend for Plumbing Contractors in 2015." November–December 2014. http://www.plumbingperspective.com/construction-outlook-positive-2015.

Scott, Gina. "Clever Ways to Answer Questions in a Job Interview," http://work.chron.com/clever-ways-answer-questions-job-interview-26744.html.

University of Chicago. "Plumbing Foreman." http://www.appa.org/jobexpress/jobsDescriptionDetail.cfm?jobid=3735.

US Bureau of Labor Statistics *Handbook.* "Plumbers, Pipefitters, and Steamfitters." http://www.bls.gov/ooh/construction-and-extraction/plumbers-pipefitters-and-steamfitters.htm#.

Welded Construction, L.P. "Pipeline Construction." http://www.welded.com/process/process.htm.

Welder's Universe. "Pipeline Construction, Pipefitting, and Plumbing." http://www.weldersuniverse.com/pipeline_construction.html.

Index

Page numbers in **boldface** are illustrations. Entries in **boldface** are glossary terms.

About the Author

Jeri Freedman has a bachelor's of arts degree from Harvard University. For fifteen years she worked for high-technology companies involved in cutting-edge technologies, including advanced semiconductors and scientific testing equipment. She is the author of more than forty young adult nonfiction books, including a number of career guides, such as *High-Tech Jobs: Software Development, Careers in Human Resources, Careers in Security, Careers in Child Care,* and *Jump-Starting a Career in Hospitals and Home Health Care,* among others.